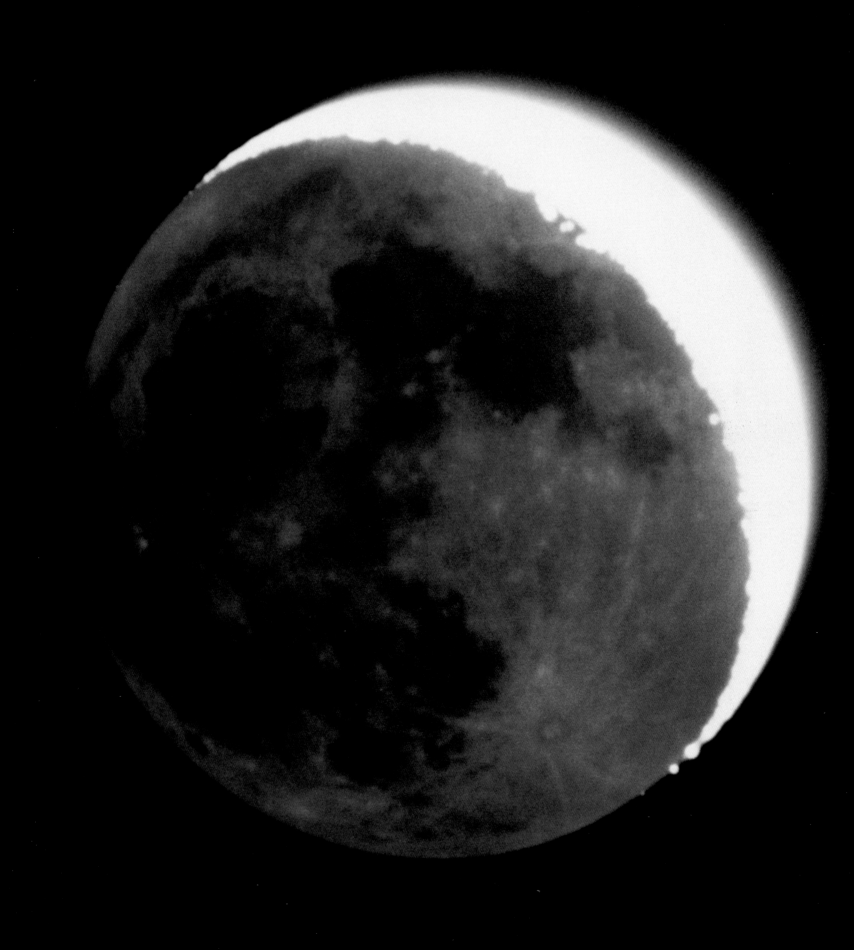

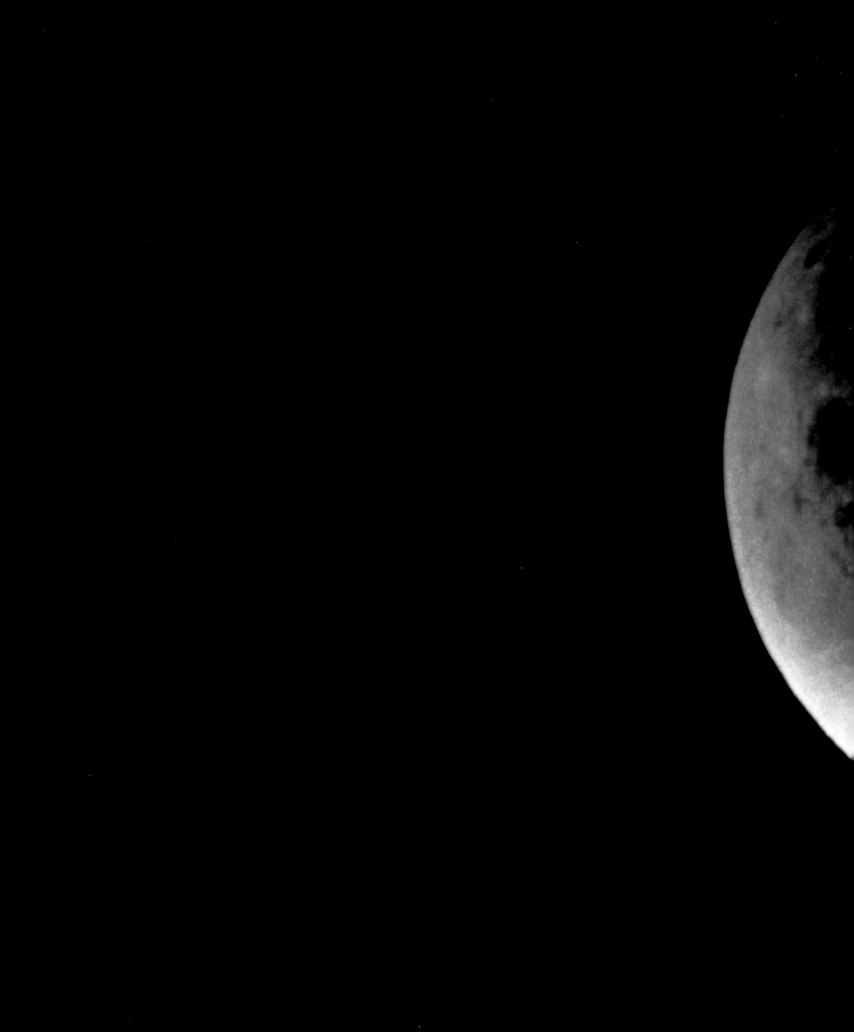

THE MOON

Michael George

CREATIVE EDUCATION

*Designed by Rita Marshall
with the help of Thomas Lawton*

*© 1992 Creative Education, Inc.
123 South Broad Street,
Mankato, Minnesota 56001*

*Photography by Devaney Stock
Photos, FPG International, NASA,
Photo Network, Photo Researchers,
Roger Ressmeyer-Starlight,
Superstock, and Visuals Unlimited*

*Library of Congress
Cataloging-in-Publication Data*

*George, Michael, 1964–
The moon / by Michael George.
    p.   cm.
Summary: Text and photographs
examine the origins, geology, and
exploration of Earth's nearest
neighbor in space.
ISBN 0-88682-436-2
[1. Moon—Juvenile literature.
2. Moon.] I. Title.   91-8221
QB582.G46   1991   CIP
523.3—dc20   AC*

In Memory of
GEORGE R. PETERSON, SR.

6

Soon after sunset on a cloudless night, the black sky above the eastern horizon turns a lighter shade of gray. The sky gradually grows brighter until the *Moon* rises above the horizon. As the Moon travels across the sky, its eerie glow causes wolves to howl and people to stare.

Moonrise.

People have gazed at the Moon since the very beginnings of humanity. For much of human history, people worshipped the Moon, thinking it was a god or a spirit. More recently, people came to realize that the Moon is a world similar, in some ways, to our own.

Like the Earth, the moon is a huge ball of material that floats through space. It is about 2,160 miles across, or about one-fourth as wide as the Earth. In the sky, the Moon appears to be about the same size as the Sun, but it is actually many times smaller. In fact, more than 50 million Moons could fit inside the Sun. The Moon seems to be about the same size as the Sun simply because it is much closer to the Earth. On average, the Moon is about two hundred and fifty thousand miles from Earth; the Sun, by comparison, is about 93 million miles away.

The Moon seen from space.

On a clear night, the Moon glows more brilliantly than the brightest star in the sky. However, like its apparent size, the Moon's brightness is also misleading. Unlike the stars, the Moon does not emit any light of its own. Instead, it *Reflects* light from the Sun. As a result, the most we can see is half of the Moon—the side that is lit by the Sun. The side that faces away from the Sun is in shadow, and cannot be seen from Earth.

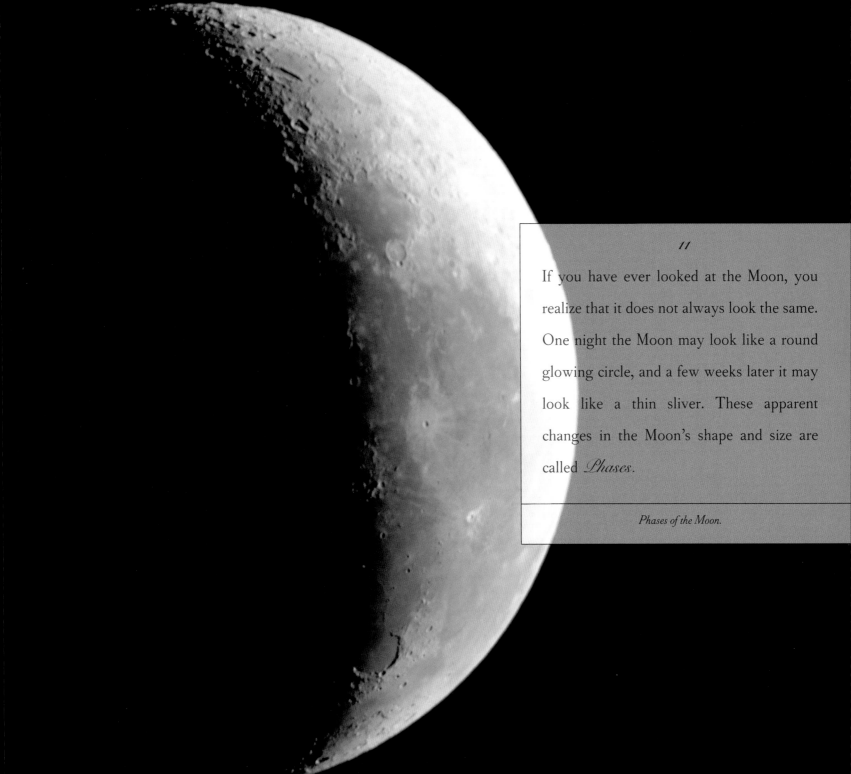

If you have ever looked at the Moon, you realize that it does not always look the same. One night the Moon may look like a round glowing circle, and a few weeks later it may look like a thin sliver. These apparent changes in the Moon's shape and size are called *Phases*.

Phases of the Moon.

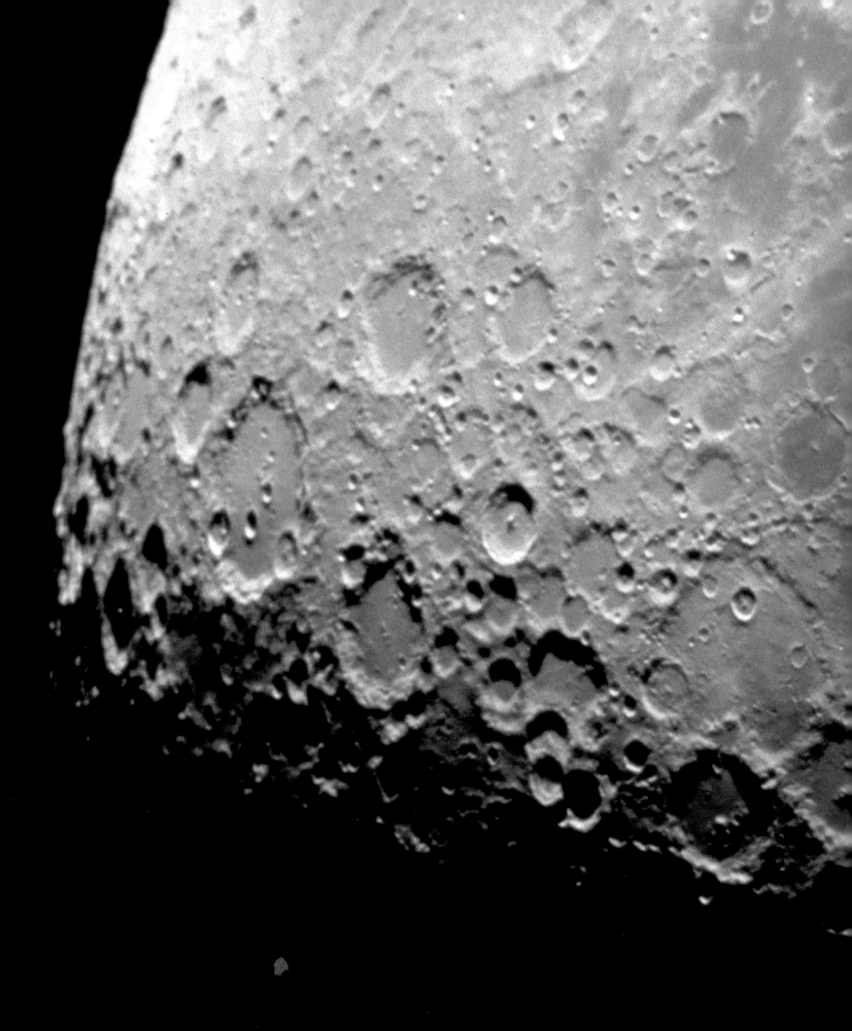

The Moon has different phases because it circles around the Earth, following a path called an *Orbit*. It takes the Moon twenty-nine and a half days to complete one orbit around the Earth. We see different amounts of the Moon's sunlit surface, and different phases, depending on the Moon's location in its orbit in relation to the Sun and Earth.

Although it is interesting to track the path of the Moon across the sky and observe its changing size and shape, it is even more fascinating to view the Moon through a telescope. With a telescope, you can actually see the surface of the Moon. Huge craters, vast plains, and bulging mountains decorate the mysterious *Lunar Landscape*.

Telescopic view of the lunar surface.

Since astronomers first peered at the Moon with telescopes, people have longed to visit its surface. In the 1960s, after centuries of dreaming and theorizing, the first human escaped our planet and ventured into space. However, before anyone could visit the Moon, scientists had to find out more about this strange other world. At the time, no one knew whether a spacecraft would land gently on the Moon's surface or disappear deep into the soil.

In order to find out more about our nearest neighbor in space, scientists sent unmanned space probes to explore the Moon. The first probes passed over the Moon but did not land on the surface. Cameras on these probes took thousands of detailed photographs of the Moon's surface. Later, several probes actually landed on the Moon and confirmed that the surface would support the weight of a manned spacecraft.

A close pass around the Moon.

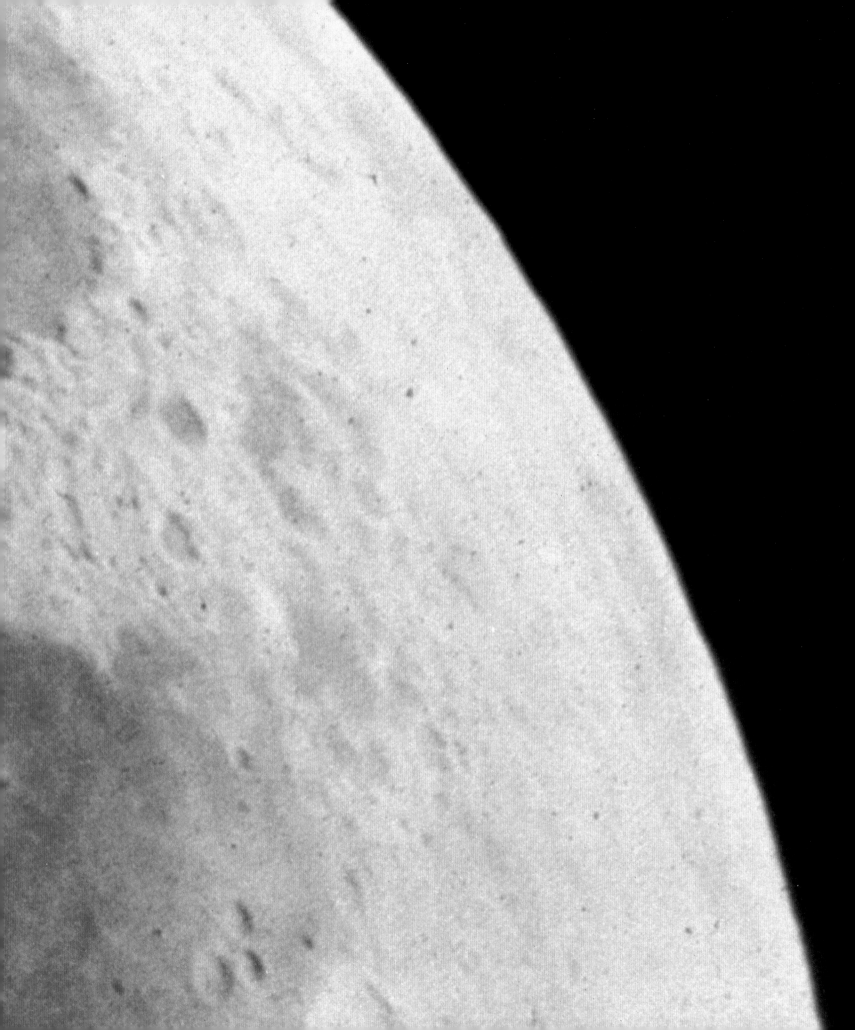

After lunar probes had explored the Moon, the United States began the Apollo space program. Despite a 1967 tragedy in which three astronauts were killed, ten successful Apollo missions paved the way for the trip that would finally place a man on the Moon. On July 19, 1969, *Apollo 11* landed on the Moon carrying two American astronauts. The next day, Neil Armstrong stepped out of the Apollo 11 lunar module and placed his foot on the surface of the Moon.

In the years that followed the historic Apollo 11 mission, six more Apollo spacecraft traveled to the Moon. By 1973, twelve Americans had left footprints on the Moon's surface. During the various missions, astronauts ran important experiments and collected materials from the lunar surface. All seven missions, including Apollo 11, returned safely to Earth.

Man steps on the Moon.

After studying the information gathered by the Apollo astronauts, scientists now have a good understanding of the Moon's past history and current conditions. Most scientists agree that the Moon was formed about 4.5 billion years ago. At this time, the Sun and the planets had just recently condensed out of a giant, swirling cloud of gas and dust. The Earth was a violent world, far different from the Earth we know today. Its surface bubbled with molten rock and seeping gases. There was no air, no water, and no life. Except for small chunks of rock and debris circling high above the surface, the Earth was without a moon.

Molten rock from a volcano.

As the Earth's surface gradually cooled and hardened, it was bombarded with bits of dust and larger bodies of rock from space. Scientists theorize that, on one fateful occasion, a chunk of material nearly half the size of the Earth crashed into the planet. The violent collision sent a glob of molten Earth flying into space. Unable to escape the Earth's gravity, the glob of material began to circle the Earth, far above the surface. Over millions of years the mass of material gradually cooled and hardened, thus forming the Moon.

Moonrise over Earth.

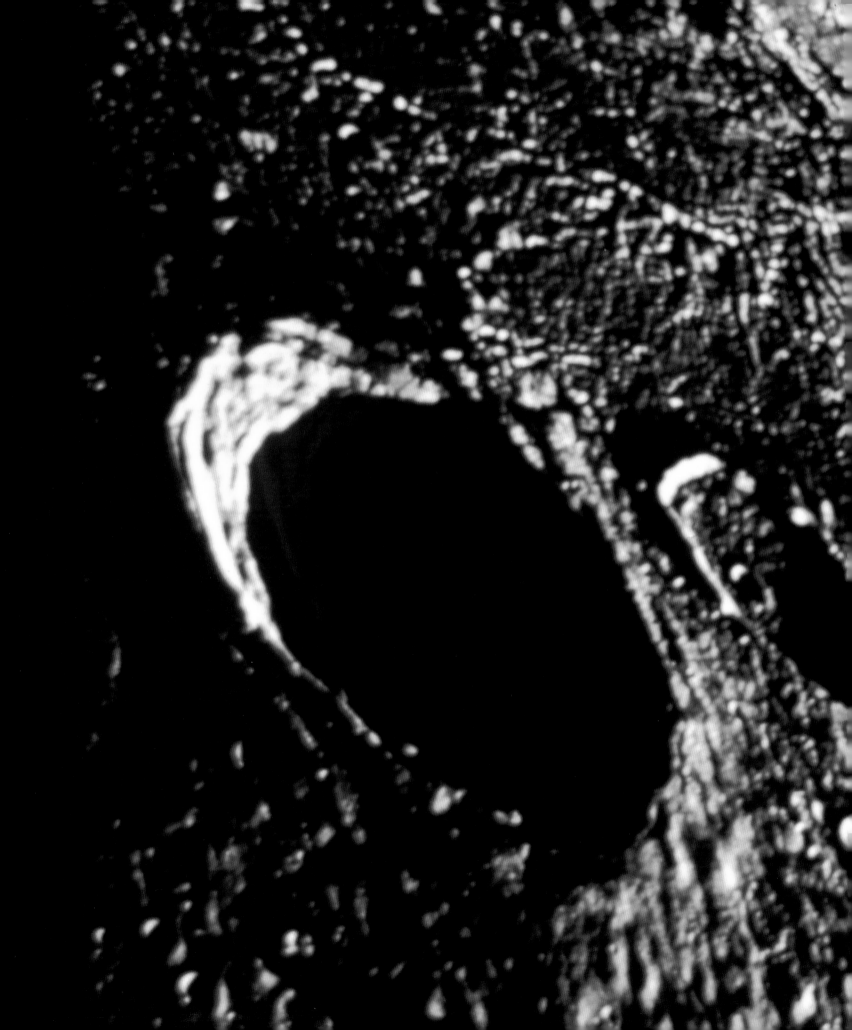

To this day, the Moon continues to circle the Earth. As the Moon travels around our planet, it also spins on its axis, similar to a twirling top. The Moon completes one *Rotation* every twenty-nine and a half days—the same length of time it takes the Moon to complete one *Revolution* around the Earth. Because of the equal timing of the Moon's rotation and revolution, we always see the same side of the Moon from Earth. The other side always faces away from the Earth, toward the vastness of space. Until probes photographed the Moon's far side, no one knew what was there.

The other side of the Moon.

Another interesting consequence of the Moon's rotation is the length of a day on the Moon. A day on Earth is twenty-four hours long. This is the time it takes the Earth to spin once on its axis. On the Moon, a complete rotation takes twenty-nine and a half days. As a result, one day on the Moon is twenty-nine and a half Earth days long— more than fourteen Earth days of sunshine and more than fourteen Earth days of darkness.

Total solar eclipse.

Besides having a much longer day, the Moon also differs from the Earth in many other ways. Unlike the Earth, the Moon is not surrounded by a layer of gases, called an *Atmosphere*. With no atmosphere, the Moon experiences no change in its weather and seasons. There are no winds, no clouds, and no rain. But the Moon is far from a sunny paradise. For one thing, there is no air to breathe on the Moon. And without a blanket of air to control temperatures, the Moon is both very hot and very cold. During the day, temperatures soar to over two hundred degrees Fahrenheit. But as soon as the Sun sinks below the horizon, the temperature plummets. In some areas, the temperature drops to four hundred degrees below zero during the long lunar night.

The Moon has no weather and no seasons.

Like its climate, the Moon's surface is very different from the Earth's. On the Moon there are no blue oceans, green meadows, or swaying trees. The Moon's surface is covered with fine, gray dust and littered with stray boulders. The lunar landscape is lifeless, silent, and still.

The most common features of the Moon's barren surface are circular holes called *Craters*. The surface of the Moon is scarred by billions of craters. There are craters connected to craters, and even craters on top of craters. Some are so small they can be seen only with a microscope, while many others are hundreds of miles wide.

Billions of craters.

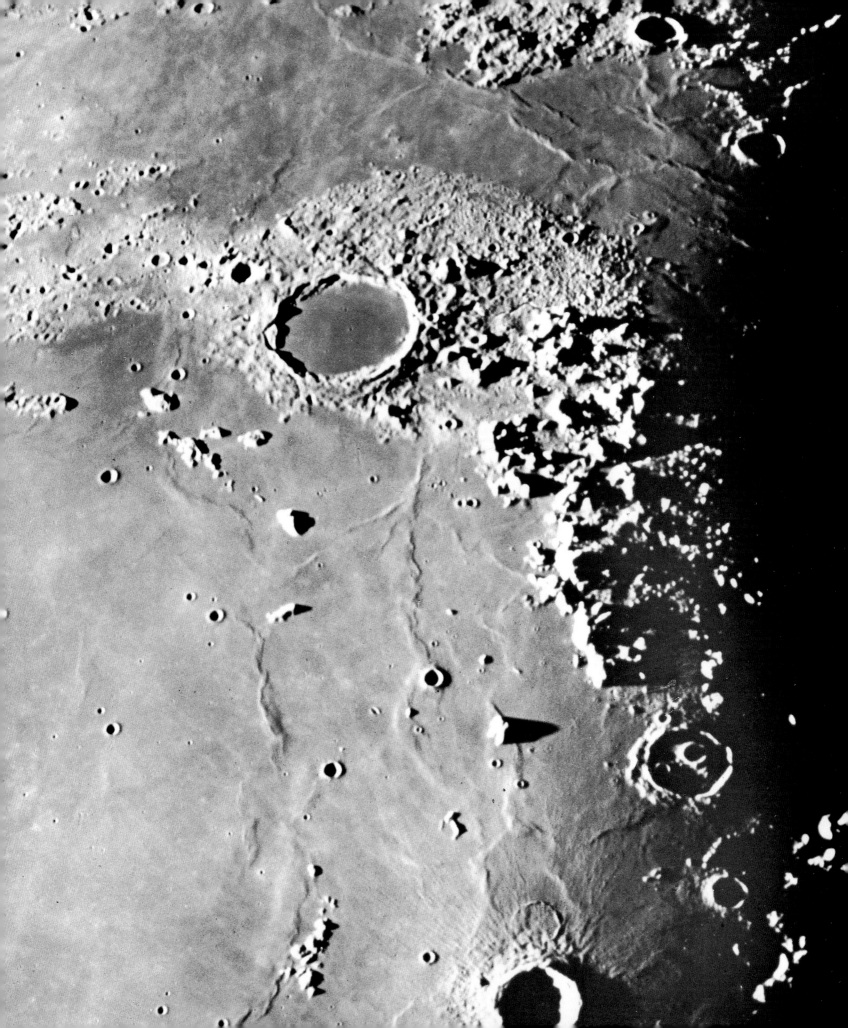

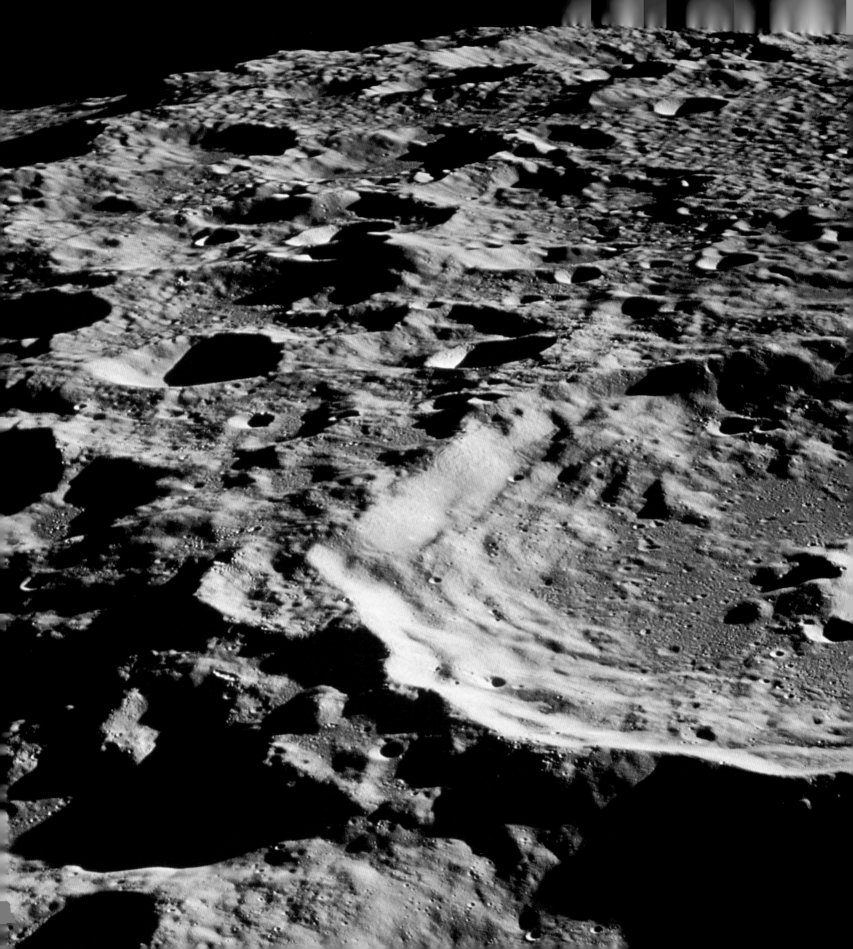

Most craters on the Moon were created when chunks of rock, called *Meteoroids,* collided with the surface. The collision between the Moon and a large meteoroid is an awesome display of nature's power. Shock waves from the thunderous collision can shake the Moon thousands of miles from the site of impact. Millions of tons of rock may be vaporized the instant contact is made. Other rocks are thrust miles above the surface as a thick cloud of dust mushrooms into the sky. After the dust settles, a circular crater marks the point of impact. Like a footprint made when you stomp your feet in thick, wet snow, a crater is much larger than the meteoroid that formed it.

Craters photographed by Apollo 11.

Although craters scar most of the Moon's surface, vast areas of the Moon are relatively smooth and crater-free. These regions, called *Maria,* can be seen from Earth as large, dark patches. The cause of the smooth lunar maria puzzled scientists for many years. Scientists now believe that most lunar craters were formed more than four billion years ago, when the Moon was very young. After being severely scarred by meteoroids, the Moon experienced a period of volcanic activity. During violent volcanic eruptions, lava flowed into low-lying plains and covered large regions of the Moon's rough, cratered surface. About three billion years ago, the interior of the Moon cooled and the lunar volcanoes stopped erupting. Since then, very few meteoroids have collided with the Moon. Therefore, the lava-filled plains are much smoother than the rest of the lunar surface.

Maria regions.

If you look closely at the full Moon, you can see light gray areas alongside the dark maria. These are mountainous regions, known as *Highlands,* which were never covered with dark lava. Some of the largest mountains on the Moon are located in the highlands. The *Leibnitz Mountains,* near the Moon's south pole, measure at least twenty-six thousand feet—as high as the tallest mountains on Earth. The highlands, however, look very different from the rough, jagged mountains on Earth. Unlike our mountains, the highlands have been worn smooth over billions of years by showers of dust and particles from space.

A lunar mountain range.

Despite its uninviting climate and barren landscape, the Moon will not remain an uninhabited wasteland for the rest of eternity. In the future, scientists may set up observatories on the Moon, in which they can study the universe. Visibility on the Moon is always excellent since there are no clouds, dust, or smog. And because the Moon rotates so slowly, objects in the sky can be observed for several hundred hours before they disappear over the horizon.

The Moon may someday be a space observatory.

If we discover valuable resources on the Moon, we may also build mining settlements there. These settlements would supply the materials needed to build and maintain permanent settlements in space. The Moon could be an important source of materials because its gravity is six times weaker than the Earth's. In other words, objects on the Moon weigh six times less than they do on Earth. Because of the Moon's weak gravity, mining and transporting lunar materials would be easier and less expensive than transporting materials from Earth.

Photo from a manned space mission.

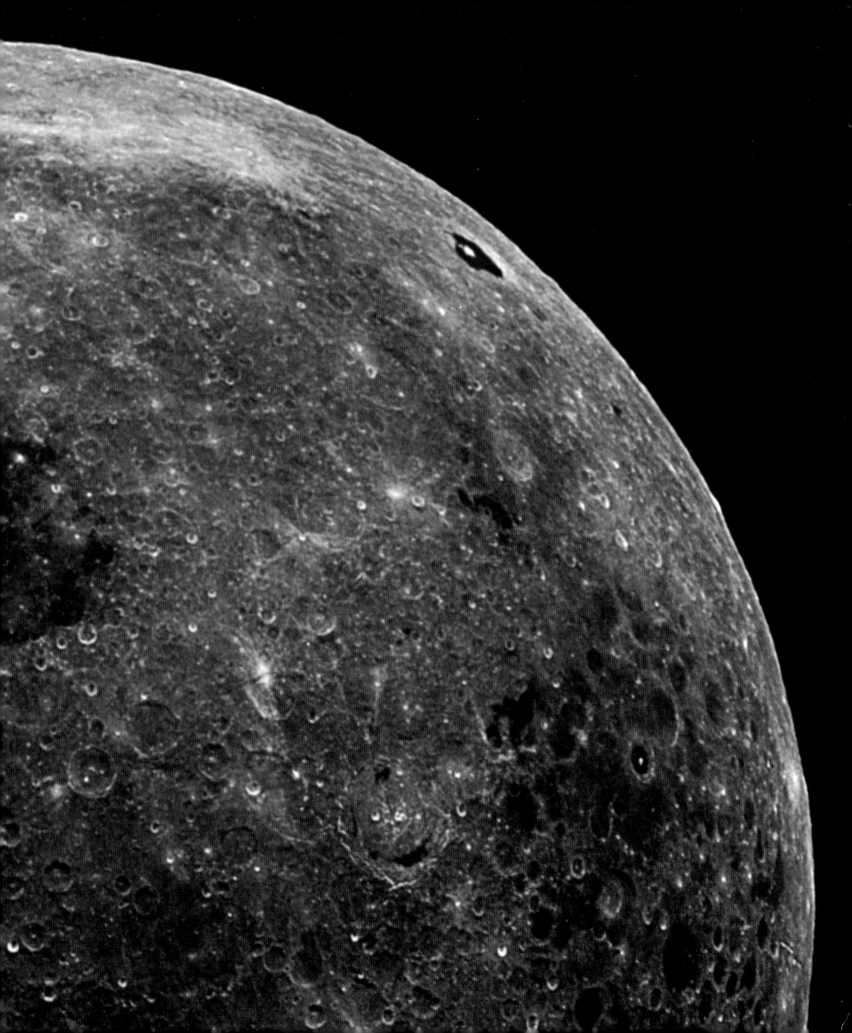

After centuries of fantasizing and theorizing about the *Moon*, and finally visiting it, we have learned much about our nearest neighbor in space. From our explorations we have learned that the Moon is a lonely world, devoid of water, color, and life. From one horizon to the other, all that is visible is the dull gray, cratered surface. Someday we may build settlements on its surface, but above the Moon's horizon, the Earth's blue oceans and white clouds will always beckon us home.

Earthrise over the Moon.